MW01204355

Easy Classical Piano & Electric Guitar Duets

Featuring music of Mozart, Beethoven, Vivaldi, Handel and other composers.
In Standard Notation and Tableture.

Easy Classical Piano & Electric Guitar Duets

Revised Edition

ISBN-13:978-1470081201
ISBN-10:1470081202

Contents

Playing guide

Notation
In this book, two methods of music notation are presented: standard notation and tablature.

Tablature
Tablature indicates the position of the notes on the fretboard. There are six lines, one for each string.

	1 Thinest
	STRINGS
	6 Thickest

The number placed on a line indicates the fret location of a note.

This indicates the 3rd fret of the first string: a G note.

This indicates the 1st fret of the second string: a C note.

This indicates the third string open: a G note.

This indicates the 4th fret of the fourth string: an F# note.

This indicates the 5th fret of the fifth string: a D note.

This indicates the sixth string open: an E note.

Standard notation
Notes are written on a Staff.

Staff
The staff consists of five lines and four spaces, on which notes symbols are placed.

Clef

A clef assigns an individual note to a certain line. The **Treble Clef** or **G Clef** is used for the Electric Guitar.

This clef indicates the position of the note G which is on the second line from the bottom.

Note

A note is a sign used to represent the relative pitch of a sound.
There are seven notes: A, B, C, D, E, F and G.

Notes on Treble Clef:

Ledger lines

The ledger lines are used to inscribe notes outside the lines and spaces of the staff.

Accidentals

An accidental is a symbol to raise or lower the pitch of a note.

♯ sharp   Next note up half step.

♭ flat   Next note down half step.

♮ natural   Cancels a flat or a sharp.

Note values

A **note value** is used to indicate the duration of a note. A **rest** is an interval of silence, marked by a sign indicating the length of the pause. Each rest corresponds to a particular note value.

o	Whole note	▬	Whole rest
♩	Half note	▬	Half rest
♩	Quarter note	♪	Quarter rest
♪	Eighth note	⁊	Eighth rest
♬	Sixteenth note	⁊	Sixteenth rest

Dotted note

A dotted note is a note with a small dot written after it. The dot adds half as much again to the basic note's duration.

Tie

A tie is a curved line connecting the heads of two notes of the same pitch, indicating that they are to be played as a single note with a duration equal to the sum of the individual notes' note values.

Bars or Measures

The staff is divided into equal segments of time consisting of the same number of beats, called bar or measures.

Time signature

Time signature consists of two numbers, the upper number specifies how many beats (or counts) are in each measure, and the lower number tells us the note value which represents one beat.

Example: 4/4 means four quarters, or four beats per measure with a quarter note receiving one beat or count.

Key signature

A Key signature is a group of accidentals, generally written at the beginning of a score immediately after the clef, and shows which notes always get sharps or flats. Accidentals on the lines and spaces in the key signature affect those notes throughout the piece unless there is a natural sign.

Repeat sign

The repeat sign indicates a section should be repeated from the beginning, and then continue on. A corresponding sign facing the other way indicates where the repeat is to begin.

Repeat Sign

First and second endings

The section should be repeated from the beginning, and number brackets above the bars indicate which to played the first time (1), which to play the second time (2).

Dynamics
Dynamics refers to the volume of the notes.

p   (piano), meaning soft.
mp   (mezzo-piano), meaning "moderately soft".
mf   (mezzo-forte), meaning "moderately loud".
f   (forte), meaning loud.

Crescendo. A gradual increase in volume.
Decrescendo. A gradual decrease in volume.

Tempo Markings
Tempo is written at the beginning of a piece of music and indicates how slow or fast this piece should be played.

Lento — very slow (40–60 bpm)
Adagio — slow and stately (66–76 bpm)
Andate — at a walking pace (76–108 bpm)
Moderato — moderately (101-110 bpm)
Allegretto — moderately fast (but less so than allegro)
Allegro — fast, quickly and bright (120–139 bpm)
Presto — extremely fast (180–200 bpm)
Alla marcia — in the manner of a march
In tempo di valse — in tempo of vals
rallentando — gradual slowing down
a tempo — returns to the base tempo after a *rallentando*

Articulation

Legato. Notes are played smoothly and connected.

Stacatto. Notes are played separated or detached from its neighbours by a silence.

Fermata (pause)
The note is to be prolonged at the pleasure of the performer.

Fingering

In this book **left hand fingering** is indicated using numbers above the staff.

0= open
1= index
2= middle
3= ring
4= little finger

Right Hand

There are two styles of playing the electric guitar: using the fingers or using the pick (plectrum). This book uses the pick, however all of the pieces can be played using the fingers.

⊓ means pick downward   ⋁ means pick upward

-Roman numbers indicates fret position for bars

CI = full bar, first fret.
cII = half bar, second fret.
Solid lines indicates how long to hold the bar.

1 8 1 2 ГОД, Op. 49

(1812 Overture)

Piotr Ilyich Tchaikovsky

An der schönen blauen Donau, Op. 314

Johann Strauss II

In Tempo di Valse

Bourrée, BWV 996

Johann Sebastian Bach

Щелкунчик, Op. 71a

(Dance of the Flowers)

Piotr Ilyich Tchaikovsky

Tempo di Valse

Eine kleine Nachtmusik, K.525

Wolfgang Amadeus Mozart

Allegro

Für Elise, WoO 59

Ludwig van Beethoven

Greensleeves

Traditional English Folk Song

Andante

Guten Abend, gut' Nacht

Johannes Brahms

I Dovregubbens hall

Edvard Grieg

Alla marcia e molto marcato

Jesus bleibet meine Freude, BWV 147

Johann Sebastian Bach

Kanon in D-Dur

Johann Pachelbel

Adagio

La Donna è Mobile

Giuseppe Verdi

Allegro - la Primavera, RV. 269

Antonio Lucio Vivaldi

Menuett, BWV Anh 114

Johann Sebastian Bach

Ode an die Freude, Op. 125

Ludwig van Beethoven

Pomp and Circumstance March Nº1, Op. 39

Edward Elgar

Molto Maestoso

Treulich geführt

Richard Wagner

Molto Vivace

Alla Hornpipe - Water Music, HWV 349

George Frideric Handel

info@marcomusica.com

Made in the USA
Coppell, TX
15 October 2021